Measurement: Grade 2

Introduction (continued)

Administer unit assessments before beginning a unit. When the unit is finished, you may use the unit assessments as posttests. The overall assessment may also be administered after a student, group of students, or the entire class has completed the book. Explain the purpose of the assessment tests to the class.

2. Explain the purpose of the worksheets to the class.

3. Review the mechanics of how you would like students to work with the activities. Will they work in pairs? Are the activities for homework?

4. Introduce the students to the process and purpose of the activities. Work with students when they have difficulty. Assign only a few pages at a time to avoid pressure.

Additional Notes

Parent Communication—Send the Letter to Parents home with students.

Student Communication—Read the Letter to Students to the class. Answer any questions that arise. Encourage students to share the letter with their parents.

Bulletin Board—Display completed worksheets or projects to show student progress.

Student Progress Chart—Duplicate the grid sheets found on pages 6–7. Record student names in the left column. Note the date of completion of each lesson for each student. If students are working independently according to individual areas of weakness, you may wish to highlight the units in which students need practice for convenient reference.

Curriculum Correlation—This chart helps you with cross-curriculum lesson planning.

Have Fun!—Working with these activities should be fun, as well as meaningful, for you and your students.

Dear Parent,

During this school year, our class will be working with measurement skills. We will be completing activity sheets that will strengthen skills in measurement. We will use estimation and measure length, capacity, temperature, and mass. We will study time and money and do computations in measurement.

From time to time, I may send home activity sheets. To help your child, please consider the following suggestions:

- Provide a quiet place to work.
- Go over the directions on the worksheet together. See that your child understands what is being asked.
- Encourage your child to do his or her best.
- Check the lesson when it is complete.
- Go over your child's work, and note improvements as well as problems.

Help your child maintain a positive attitude about mathematics. Let your child know that each lesson provides an opportunity to have fun and to learn. If your child expresses anxiety about the work, talk to your child about ways to eliminate these feelings. Your relaxed attitude and support will help to reduce your child's anxiety.

Enjoy this time that you spend with your child. With your help, his or her skills will improve with each activity completed.

Thank you for your support!

Cordially,

Measurement: Grade 2

Table of Contents

Measurement: Grade 2

Introduction

Teachers are well aware of the importance of developing strong mathematics skills in their students. Students, on the other hand, may not understand how math will be a useful tool outside of school. That is why application of math skills, once mastered, to real-life situations is vital to students' appreciation of math.

Mathematics skills are used in almost every aspect of our lives, from an early age. Students may not realize that they are using math skills when they build, draw, cook, or score a game. By showing them that these skills do relate to math, teachers and parents can help students make the connection.

Measurement is one of the most common ways that students will use mathematics, both as students and as adults. From dressing for the weather to coming home on time or spending allowances, students estimate and use measurement skills throughout their day.

The National Council for Teachers of Mathematics (NTCM) has set standards for mathematical content and the processes through which students should gain and use their knowledge. Measurement is one of the five content areas set forth in the standards. In the second grade, students should use a variety of tools and techniques to measure, apply the results in problem-solving situations, and communicate the reasoning used in solving these problems. This book provides opportunities for learning measurement concepts in accordance with the NCTM standards.

Organization

Measurement is divided into eight units covering estimation, length, capacity, temperature, mass, time, money, and computation in measurement. Each unit provides opportunities for hands-on learning, as well as applications to real-life situations. Students use estimation skills and then prove their measurements. Part of each unit is devoted to metric measurements. Tools needed for hands-on activities are listed on the bottom of the page.

Each unit in *Measurement* is preceded by an assessment for that unit. There is also an overall assessment that covers all of the measurement skills in the book. Each of the tests can be used as a pretest to gauge students' areas of strength or weakness, as well as a posttest to demonstrate what students have learned. The overall test can be used as a pretest to give the teacher a clearer picture of the units in which students need the most practice. It can also be used as a posttest to demonstrate improvement or highlight areas that still require attention.

Use

Measurement is designed to complement existing math programs. It is intended for independent use by students who have had instruction in the specific skills covered in the lessons. Copies of the activity sheets can be given to individuals, pairs of students, or groups of students for completion. When students are familiar with the content of the worksheets, they can be assigned as homework.

Determine the implementation that best fits your students' needs and your classroom structure. The following plan suggests a format for implementation.

1. Administer the overall assessment to establish baseline information on each student. You may choose to concentrate on certain units after reviewing the test results.

Dear Student,

An important part of what we do this year in math will be working with measurement. You use measurement many times each day. You may not even think about it. You check the weather. You look at the time. You may buy a lunch. These are all measurement skills. Measurement is math!

The activities in this book will be fun. You will see how useful measurement is. The worksheets will help you practice. Then, you will use your skills in real-life ways.

When you complete a worksheet, remember to:

• Read the directions carefully. What are you being asked to do?
• Read each question carefully. All the questions on a page may not be the same.
• Check your answers when you are finished.

Have fun as you measure your way through math!

Sincerely,

Measurement: Grade 2

Student Progress Chart

STUDENT NAME	UNIT 1 ESTIMATION								UNIT 2 LENGTH												UNIT 3 CAPACITY								UNIT 4 TEMPERATURE							
	13	14	15	16	17	18	19	20	21	22	23	24	25	26	27	28	29	30	31	32	33	34	35	36	37	38	39	40	41	42	43	44	45	46	47	48

www.svschoolsupply.com

© Steck-Vaughn Company

Measurement 2, SV 2066-4

Measurement: Grade 2

Student Progress Chart, p. 2

STUDENT NAME	UNIT 5 MASS 49 50 51 52 53 54 55 56	UNIT 6 TIME 57 58 59 60 61 62 63 64 65 66 67 68 69 70	UNIT 7 MONEY 71 72 73 74 75 76 77 78 79 80 81 82	UNIT 8 COMPUTATION 83 84 85 86 87 88 89 90 91 92 93 94

Measurement: Grade 2

Curriculum Correlation

	Science	Art	Language Arts
Unit 1: Estimation			20
Unit 2: Length			32
Unit 3: Capacity			39, 40
Unit 4: Temperature	43, 44, 45, 46, 47, 48	44, 45	46, 47, 48
Unit 5: Mass			53, 56
Unit 6: Time		63	60, 61, 62, 63, 66, 67, 68, 69
Unit 7: Money			76, 77, 78, 79, 80, 81, 82
Unit 8: Computation		92	89, 90, 93

Name _____ Date _____

Overall Assessment
Measurement: Grade 2

DIRECTIONS

Read each question. Darken the circle by the correct answer.

Unit 1: Estimation

1. What would you use to measure length?

Ⓐ a cup

Ⓑ a ruler

Ⓒ a clock

2. Which of these would be the weight of a mouse?

Ⓐ 2 ounces

Ⓑ 2 pounds

Ⓒ 16 ounces

3. A boy is most likely 4 _____ tall.

Ⓐ yards

Ⓑ feet

Ⓒ inches

Unit 2: Length

4. How long is a pencil?

Ⓐ 6 yards

Ⓑ 6 feet

Ⓒ 6 inches

5. Which of these is between 1 inch and 2 inches?

Ⓐ $2\frac{1}{2}$ inches

Ⓑ $1\frac{3}{4}$ inches

Ⓒ $\frac{1}{2}$ inch

6. Jim has 8 centimeters of tape. He uses half of it to wrap a gift. How much tape does Jim have left?

Ⓐ 2 centimeters

Ⓑ 4 centimeters

Ⓒ 6 centimeters

Go on to the next page.

Name _____ Date _____

Overall Assessment
Measurement: Grade 2, p. 2

DIRECTIONS

Read each question. Darken the circle by the correct answer.

Unit 3: Capacity

7. Julie shares glue with 3 friends. She gives them 10 mL of glue each. How much glue does Julie share?

  Ⓐ 30 mL

  Ⓑ 1 L

  Ⓒ 3 mL

8. Maggie has a $\frac{1}{2}$-cup measure. How many measures will she need to make 2 cups?

  Ⓐ 2

  Ⓑ 4

  Ⓒ 8

9. Ed drank 3 cups of milk from 1 quart. How much is left?

  Ⓐ 1 cup

  Ⓑ 2 cups

  Ⓒ 1 pint

Unit 4: Temperature

10. It is 30° F today. It is _____.

  Ⓐ hot

  Ⓑ warm

  Ⓒ cold

11. The Flint family is going swimming at the beach. It is most likely _____.

  Ⓐ 88° F

  Ⓑ 57° F

  Ⓒ 23° F

12. What is the temperature on this thermometer?

  Ⓐ 45° F

  Ⓑ 48° F

  Ⓒ 48° C

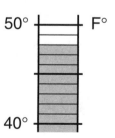

Go on to the next page.

Overall Assessment
Measurement: Grade 2, p. 3

Unit 5: Mass

13. Which of these would be the weight of an apple?

Ⓐ 32 ounces

Ⓑ 16 ounces

Ⓒ 4 ounces

14. Which of these would weigh 5 kilograms?

Ⓐ a bag of dog food

Ⓑ an orange

Ⓒ a man

15. June's cat weighs half as much as her puppy. Her puppy weighs 4 pounds. How much does her cat weigh?

Ⓐ 4 ounces

Ⓑ 2 ounces

Ⓒ 2 pounds

Unit 6: Time

16. What is the time on this clock?

Ⓐ 3:00

Ⓑ 2:00

Ⓒ 1:00

17. What is the time on this clock?

5:45

Ⓐ 15 minutes before 6

Ⓑ 15 minutes after 6

Ⓒ 45 minutes before 5

18. About how long does it take to eat lunch?

Ⓐ 1 hour

Ⓑ 45 minutes

Ⓒ 30 minutes

Go on to the next page.

Overall Assessment
Measurement: Grade 2, p. 4

DIRECTIONS

Read each question. Darken the circle by the correct answer.

Unit 7: Money

19. Meg has 2 quarters. Can she buy an apple that sells for 45 cents?

Ⓐ No, she needs more money.

Ⓑ Yes, she has an extra 5 cents.

Ⓒ Yes, she has the exact amount.

20. Greg found 2 dimes and 1 nickel on the ground. How much did he find?

Ⓐ 30 cents

Ⓑ 20 cents

Ⓒ 25 cents

21. Joe's 5 friends each gave him 1 cent. Which coin could Joe trade for?

Ⓐ a nickel

Ⓑ a dime

Ⓒ a quarter

Unit 8: Computation

22. What is the perimeter of this shape?

Ⓐ 8 inches

Ⓑ 13 inches

Ⓒ 16 inches

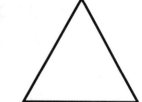

5 in.

3 in.   3 in.

5 in.

23. This triangle is 3 centimeters on each side. What is its perimeter?

Ⓐ 9 centimeters

Ⓑ 6 centimeters

Ⓒ 3 centimeters

24. How many cubic units are in this figure?

Ⓐ 1 cubic unit

Ⓑ 7 cubic units

Ⓒ 3 cubic units

Name _____ Date _____

Unit 1 Assessment
Estimation

DIRECTIONS
Read each question. Darken the circle by the correct answer.

1. What would you use to tell the temperature?
   - Ⓐ a ruler
   - Ⓑ a thermometer
   - Ⓒ a scale

2. What units would you use to measure a piece of rope?
   - Ⓐ cups
   - Ⓑ pounds
   - Ⓒ feet

3. How long would it take you to brush your teeth?
   - Ⓐ 1 hour
   - Ⓑ 3 minutes
   - Ⓒ 15 minutes

4. It is snowing outside. It is most likely _____.
   - Ⓐ 60° F
   - Ⓑ 30° F
   - Ⓒ 85° F

Go on to the next page.

Unit 1 Assessment
Estimation, p. 2

DIRECTIONS

Read each question. Darken the circle by the correct answer.

5. James has 1 quart of orange juice. He will pour 1 cup into each glass. How many glasses can he fill?

   Ⓐ 4

   Ⓑ 2

   Ⓒ 8

6. Carlos has 80¢. The candy he wants costs 20¢ each. How many can he buy?

   Ⓐ 3

   Ⓑ 5

   Ⓒ 4

7. A wagon can hold 80 pounds. Jeff weighs 40 pounds. Julia weighs 35 pounds. Charles weighs 50 pounds. Which 2 children can ride in the wagon together?

   Ⓐ Jeff and Charles

   Ⓑ Julia and Charles

   Ⓒ Jeff and Julia

8. Jason has a soccer game in half an hour. Which thing does he have time to do before his game?

   Ⓐ watch a movie

   Ⓑ read some of his book

   Ⓒ make a cake

Name _____ Date _____

What Should You Use?

DIRECTIONS

Draw a line to show the best measure for each activity.

1.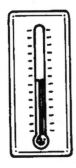

a.

2.

b.

3.

c.

4.

d.

What Do You Think?

Estimate to solve these problems.

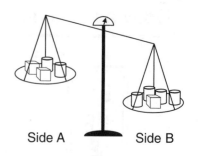

1. Which side of the balance weighs more?
   Circle <u>A</u> or <u>B</u>.

   A   B

2. Greg looks at the thermometer.
   What clothes will he wear?

   Coat   Swimsuit

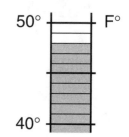

3. Sam has 1 quart of milk. He drinks 1 cup
   of it. Does he have more or less than 1 pint left?
   Circle <u>More</u> or <u>Less</u>.

   More   Less

4. Lani has a ribbon that is 16 centimeters
   long. Can she cut 2 pieces that are
   9 centimeters long? Circle <u>Yes</u> or <u>No</u>.

   Yes   No

How Long Does It Take?

DIRECTIONS

Circle how much time each activity takes.

1. making a bed

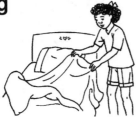

more than 1 hour
about 10 minutes
about 1 hour

2. seeing a movie

more than 1 hour
about 10 minutes
about 1 hour

3. one lesson at school

more than 1 hour
about 10 minutes
about 1 hour

4. watering plants

more than 1 hour
about 10 minutes
about 1 hour

5. playing a game with a friend

more than 1 hour
about 10 minutes
about 1 hour

6. hearing a story

more than 1 hour
about 10 minutes
about 1 hour

Name _____ Date _____

How Far Around?

DIRECTIONS

Look at each shape. Circle your estimate.

1.

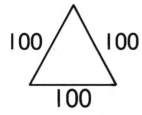

The perimeter is (< 400) > 400.

2.

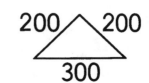

The perimeter is < 500   > 500.

3.

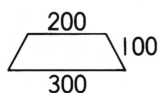

The perimeter is < 500   > 500.

4.

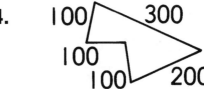

The perimeter is < 900   > 900.

DIRECTIONS

These shapes have equal sides. Circle your guess.

5.

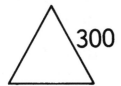

The perimeter is < 800   > 800.

6.

The perimeter is < 400   > 400.

7.

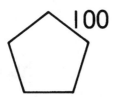

The perimeter is < 600   > 600.

8.

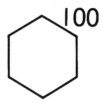

The perimeter is < 800   > 800.

Name _____   Date _____

How Many Will Fit?

DIRECTIONS

How many 1-inch squares will fit in each space?
First, write your guess. Then, use 1-inch squares to check.

1.

Guess. _____ squares   Check. _____ squares

2.

Guess. _____ squares   Check. _____ squares

3.

Guess. _____ squares

Check. _____ squares

Tools: 1-inch counting cubes

Name _____ Date _____

Marble-ous!

A store is having a contest. You win a prize if you guess how many marbles are in the jar. How could you guess the number of marbles in the jar without counting them?

_____

_____

_____

_____

Ask your teacher to fill a jar with marbles for your classroom. Get a shoe box, and make a hole in the top. Have a contest to see who can guess the closest to the number of marbles. The winner gets the marbles!

Put your name and your guess on a piece of paper. Put your paper in the shoe box.

Tools: clear jar, marbles, shoe box, tape

Name _____ Date _____

Unit 2 Assessment
Length

DIRECTIONS
Read each question. Darken the circle by the correct answer.

1. What is on a ruler between 1 inch and 2 inches?
   Ⓐ $2\frac{1}{2}$ inches
   Ⓑ $1\frac{1}{2}$ inches
   Ⓒ $\frac{1}{2}$ inch

2. Which of these is longer than 3 inches, but shorter than 5 inches?
   Ⓐ 4 inches
   Ⓑ 2 inches
   Ⓒ $5\frac{1}{2}$ inches

3. Your thumb is most likely _____ long.
   Ⓐ 5 centimeters
   Ⓑ 12 centimeters
   Ⓒ 2 centimeters

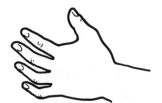

4. Bart needs 4 feet of wood to make 1 shelf. How many feet will he need to make 2 shelves?
   Ⓐ 12 feet
   Ⓑ 8 feet
   Ⓒ 2 feet

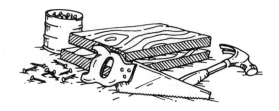

Go on to the next page.

Unit 2 Assessment
Length, p. 2

DIRECTIONS

Read each question. Darken the circle by the correct answer.

5. Jackie needs 10 inches of string to make 1 necklace. How many necklaces can she make with 50 inches of string?

Ⓐ 50 necklaces

Ⓑ 10 necklaces

Ⓒ 5 necklaces

6. It is 100 feet from the house to the well. If Tia walks halfway to the well, how far does she go?

Ⓐ 50 inches

Ⓑ 50 feet

Ⓒ 25 feet

7. Kip's pencil box is 16 centimeters long. His new pencils are 20 centimeters long. How many more centimeters long are Kip's new pencils than his box?

Ⓐ 4 centimeters

Ⓑ 2 centimeters

Ⓒ 8 centimeters

8. Karen is half as tall as her older brother, Ben. Ben is 6 feet tall. How tall is Karen?

Ⓐ 5 feet tall

Ⓑ 3 feet tall

Ⓒ 2 feet tall

This Tool Rules!

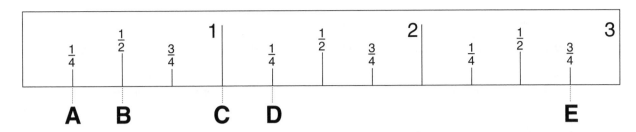

This is a section of a customary ruler. It measures length. Look at the markings on the ruler. The ruler is divided into inches. Each inch is divided into halves and quarters.

- The **A** above shows $\frac{1}{4}$ of 1 inch.
- The **B** above shows $\frac{1}{2}$ of 1 inch.
- The **C** above shows 1 inch exactly.
- The **D** above shows 1 and $\frac{1}{4}$ inches. It is past the 1-inch mark, so it is $1\frac{1}{4}$ inches.
- What do you think the **E** shows? Is it greater than 1 inch? Is it greater than 2 inches? How many quarter inches does it show? If you said $2\frac{3}{4}$ inches, you are correct.

DIRECTIONS

Look at the ruler below. For each letter, write the measurement that is shown.

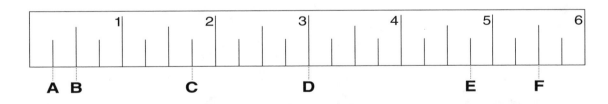

A. _____ B. _____ C. _____ D. _____ E. _____ F. _____

Go on to the next page.

www.svschoolsupply.com

© Steck-Vaughn Company

Unit 2: Length: Using a Ruler

Measurement 2, SV 2066-4

This Tool Rules!, p. 2

DIRECTIONS

Use a customary ruler to measure the length of each item.
Write the answer on the line.

1.

_____

2.

_____

3.

_____

4.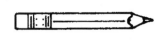

_____

5.

_____

6.

_____

7.

_____

8.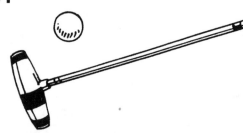

_____

9.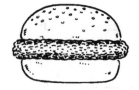

_____

10.

_____

Tool: customary ruler

Name _____   Date _____

Donna's Dollhouse

The ruler above shows inches and half inches.

DIRECTIONS

Try to guess the length of each item in Donna's dollhouse. Write your guess. Then, use a ruler to measure its length. Write the measurement.

1.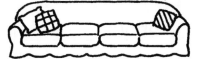

about _____ inches

exactly _____ inches

2.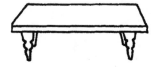

about _____ inches

exactly _____ inches

3.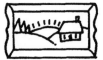

about _____ inches

exactly _____ inches

4.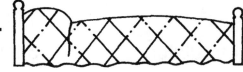

about _____ inches

exactly _____ inches

5.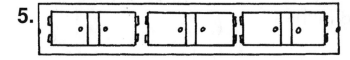

about _____ inches

exactly _____ inches

Tool: customary ruler

Name _____ Date _____

Take a Guess

DIRECTIONS

Circle the best answer. Then, use an inch ruler to measure the length to the nearest inch. Write the length.

		Estimate	**Measure**

1.

a book

Estimate
1 inch
10 inches
20 inches

Measure
about _____ inches

2.

your thumb

2 inches
9 inches
15 inches

about _____ inches

3.

a calculator

25 inches
15 inches
5 inches

about _____ inches

DIRECTIONS

Solve this problem.

4. David draws a picture that is 7 inches tall. His frame is 8 inches tall. Will the picture fit? Circle Yes or No.

Yes   No

Tool: customary ruler

Brushing Up on Measuring

DIRECTIONS

Use a small paper clip to measure each brush. Write the length.

1.

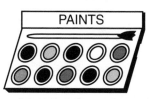

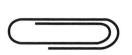

about _____ clips

2.

about _____ clips

3.

about _____ clips

4.

about _____ clips

DIRECTIONS

Solve this problem.

5. Circle the longer box.

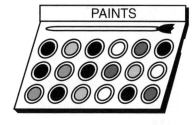

| **Tool: small paper clip** |

Name _____ Date _____

Inching Along

Use an inch ruler to draw pieces of yarn.

1. $2\frac{1}{2}$ inches

2. 5 inches

3. $3\frac{1}{4}$ inches

Solve this problem.

4. Rhonda needs $4\frac{3}{4}$ inches of ribbon.
Draw a line to show where she will cut.

Tool: customary ruler

Name _____ Date _____

String It Along

DIRECTIONS
Use your centimeter ruler to draw pieces of string.

1. 7 centimeters

2. 3 centimeters

3. 10 centimeters

DIRECTIONS
Write a number sentence, and solve.

4. Anita needs 12 centimeters of ribbon
for a craft project. If she makes 2 projects,
how much ribbon will Anita need?

_____ _____ centimeters

Tool: centimeter ruler

Name _____   Date _____

Great Goats!

DIRECTIONS
Eight goats are trying to reach the top of the mountain. Look at the numbers on the chart. Write the answer.

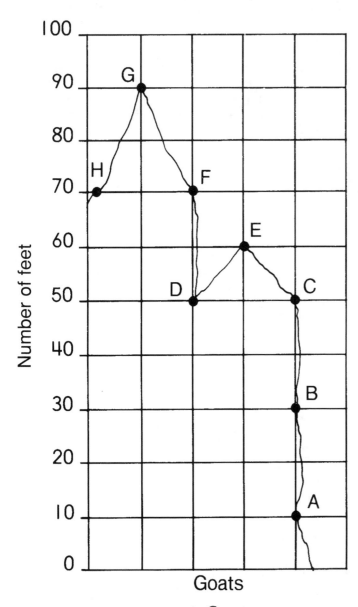

1. Where is goat C?

at 50 feet
_____

2. Where is G?

_____

3. How far is A from B?

_____

4. If F went back 20 feet, where would F be?

_____

5. What is the distance between goats A and F?

_____

6. How far is H from the bottom of the mountain?

_____

Camp Out

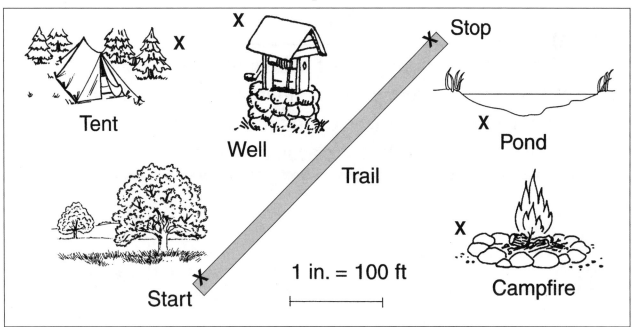

DIRECTIONS

The scale shows distance on a map. Look at the scale on this map. Use the scale and your ruler. Write how many feet there are from:

1. the tent to the start of the trail.

_____ feet

2. the campfire to the well.

_____ feet

3. the tent to the pond.

_____ feet

4. the pond to the campfire.

_____ feet

5. the end of the trail to the pond.

_____ feet

Tool: customary ruler

What a Whale!

DIRECTIONS

The blue whale is the largest animal of all. It is as long as nine of these cars in a row. What other things might be as big or long as a blue whale? Draw pictures of things you think of. Compare your ideas with your classmates' ideas.

Unit 3 Assessment
Capacity

DIRECTIONS

Read each question. Darken the circle by the correct answer.

1. A glass of juice is most likely _____.
   Ⓐ 1 cup
   Ⓑ 1 quart
   Ⓒ 1 gallon

2. Louis collected about 7 drops of water in a cup. He had collected about _____ of water.
   Ⓐ 1 liter
   Ⓑ 1 milliliter
   Ⓒ 1 kiloliter

3. There are _____ cups in 1 gallon.
   Ⓐ 4
   Ⓑ 8
   Ⓒ 16

4. Carla sold cups of lemonade for 10 cents each. She made only 40 cents. How much lemonade did Carla sell?
   Ⓐ 2 gallons
   Ⓑ 2 pints
   Ⓒ 2 quarts

Go on to the next page.

Name _____ Date _____

Unit 3 Assessment
Capacity, p. 2

DIRECTIONS

Read each question. Darken the circle by the correct answer.

5. Mr. Smith wanted to know how much water was in his pool. He used to _____ measure the water.

Ⓐ liters

Ⓑ milliliters

Ⓒ kiloliters

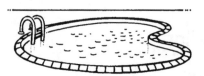

6. Four quarts is the same as _____.

Ⓐ 1 gallon

Ⓑ 2 pints

Ⓒ 8 cups

7. Jean has 3 cups of milk. She needs 1 quart. How much more does she need?

Ⓐ 1 pint

Ⓑ 1 teaspoon

Ⓒ 1 cup

8. Dan wants to save 1 gallon of soup. He has dishes that hold 1 quart each. How many dishes will he have to use to save all of the soup?

Ⓐ 3 dishes

Ⓑ 5 dishes

Ⓒ 4 dishes

Name _____ Date _____

Every Drop Counts!

DIRECTIONS

Use the water and the measures to complete each sentence.

1. There are _____
   $\frac{1}{2}$ teaspoons in a teaspoon.

2. There are _____
   pints in a quart.

3. There are _____
   quarts in a gallon.

4. There are _____
   cups in a pint.

5. There are _____
   cups in a gallon.

6. There are _____
   teaspoons in a tablespoon.

7. There are _____
   pints in a gallon.

8. There are _____
   cups in a quart.

9. There are _____
   $\frac{1}{4}$ cups in a cup.

10. There are _____
    $\frac{1}{2}$ cups in a cup.

Tools: sink or bucket of water; gallon jug, quart container, pint container (or graduated gallon container), set of measuring cups, set of measuring spoons

Name _____ Date _____

Fill 'er Up!

Circle the better estimate.

1.

more than 1 quart
less than 1 quart

2.

about 1 gallon
less than 1 gallon

Color the cups to show the same amount.

3.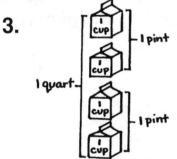

Pint

4.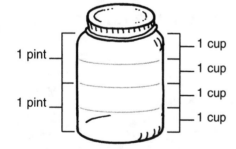

Quart

Solve this problem.

5. Marta has 1 quart of juice.
How many cups can she fill?

_____ cups

How Do They Compare?

Name _____ Date _____

DIRECTIONS

Look at each set of pictures.
Write the answer.

1. _____ cups = _____ pint   _____ pints = _____ quart

_____ quarts = _____ gallon

DIRECTIONS

In each row, circle the group of containers that holds more.

2. 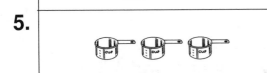	**a.**	**b.**
3.	**a.**	**b.**
4.	**a.**	**b.**
5.	**a.**	**b.**

Metric Measures

Use the water and the measures to complete each sentence about milliliters (mL) and liters (L).

1. There are _____ mL in 1 L.   **2.** There are _____ mL in $\frac{1}{2}$ L.

3. There are _____ mL in 2 L.   **4.** There are _____ mL in $\frac{1}{4}$ L.

5. A kiloliter (kL) is 1,000 liters. When do you think you would need a kL of water? _____

Look at each picture. Which unit of measure would you use to find the amount of liquid in each picture? Write <u>mL</u>, <u>L</u>, or <u>kL</u>.

6.

a can of soup

_____

7.

a carton of milk

_____

8.

a bottle of ink

_____

9.

a thimble of water

_____

10.

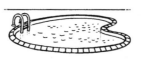

a swimming pool

_____

11.

a bottle of soda

_____

Tools: water; 2-liter bottle with markings at $\frac{1}{4}$ and $\frac{1}{2}$ liter; measure with mL markings

Name _____ Date _____

Be a Problem Solver!

DIRECTIONS

Solve each problem.

1. James has 1 gallon of milk. He uses 1 quart to make breakfast. How many quarts does he have left?

_____

2. Carlos pours 1 cup of juice from a quart carton. How many cups does he have left?

_____

3. Susan boils 1 quart of water. She uses 1 pint of the water to make tea. How many pints are left in the kettle?

_____

4. There are 4 quarts of stew in a pot. How many gallons of stew are in the pot?

_____

A Juicy Question

DIRECTIONS

You want to make 1 gallon of juice. With an 8-ounce cup, how can you find out if your pitcher will be big enough to make all of the juice?

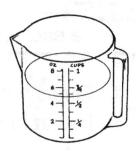

Name _____ Date _____

Unit 4 Assessment
Temperature

DIRECTIONS

Look at each picture. Darken the circle by the correct temperature.

1.

   Ⓐ 40° F
   Ⓑ 80° F
   Ⓒ 25° F

2.

   Ⓐ 33° F
   Ⓑ 45° F
   Ⓒ 72° F

3.

   Ⓐ 15° F
   Ⓑ 48° F
   Ⓒ 70° F

4.

   Ⓐ 0° C
   Ⓑ 10° C
   Ⓒ 25° C

Go on to the next page.

Name _____ Date _____

Unit 4 Assessment
Temperature, p. 2

DIRECTIONS

Read each thermometer. Darken the circle by the correct temperature.

5.

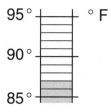

    Ⓐ 58°
    Ⓑ 55°
    Ⓒ 54°

6.

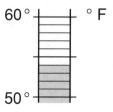

    Ⓐ 85°
    Ⓑ 87°
    Ⓒ 89°

7.

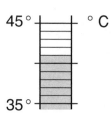

    Ⓐ 41°
    Ⓑ 38°
    Ⓒ 40°

8.

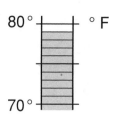

    Ⓐ 77°
    Ⓑ 79°
    Ⓒ 80°

Name _____   Date _____

Hot and Cold

DIRECTIONS

Circle the better estimate.

1.

        30 degrees Fahrenheit

        80 degrees Fahrenheit

2.

        40 degrees Fahrenheit

        90 degrees Fahrenheit

3.

        20 degrees Fahrenheit

        70 degrees Fahrenheit

4.

        50 degrees Fahrenheit

        90 degrees Fahrenheit

DIRECTIONS

Answer the question.

5. Read the thermometer. What are some activities you could do outside?

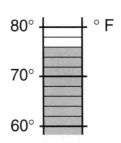

_____

_____

What Would You Do?

Color in the thermometer to show the temperature. Then, draw a picture of something that you would do at that temperature.

1.

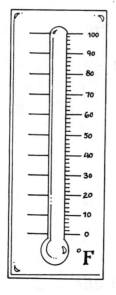

86° F

2.

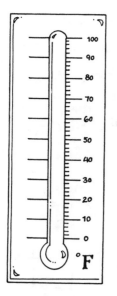

34° F

Go on to the next page.

Name _____   Date _____

What Would You Do?, p. 2

DIRECTIONS

Color in the thermometer to show the temperature. Then, draw a picture of something that you would do at that temperature.

3.

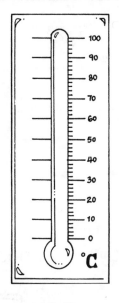

4° C

4.

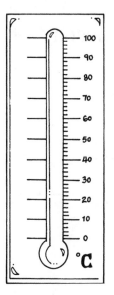

32° C

Name _____ Date _____

Weather Watch

DIRECTIONS

Mrs. Ruiz wrote the temperature each day. She started this line graph. Read the sentences, and complete the graph.

Temperature

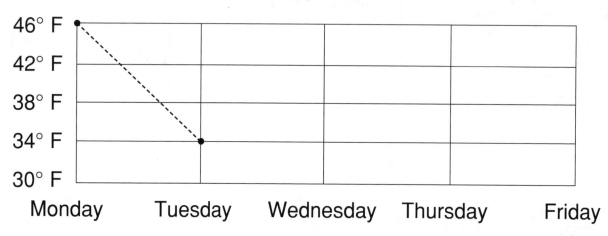

On Wednesday, the temperature was 36° F.
On Thursday, the temperature went up 2° F.
On Friday, the temperature was the same as on Tuesday.

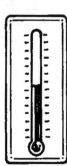

DIRECTIONS

Use the graph to answer these questions.

1. On which day was the temperature the highest?

_____

2. Was it warmer on Tuesday or on Thursday?

_____

3. Was it colder on Monday or on Wednesday?

_____

Name _____ Date _____

A Difference of Degrees

High Temperatures

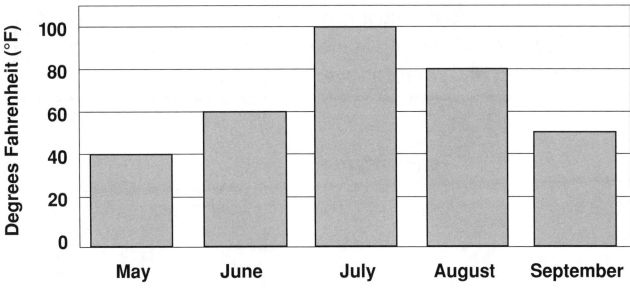

Use the graph to answer these questions.

1. What is the title of this graph?

_____

2. How many months are shown?

_____

3. What was the coolest month?

_____

4. What was the hottest month?

_____

5. How much warmer was it in August than in June?

_____

6. How much cooler was it in September than in July?

_____

Keep Track of the Temperature

DIRECTIONS

You may do this activity on a weekend when you are at home. Look at a thermometer in the morning. Look at the thermometer at noon, and again in the late afternoon. Write the temperatures that you see in the chart each time. Do the same thing the next day. Then, answer the questions.

Temperatures

Day	Morning	Noon	Late Afternoon

1. At what time of day was the temperature the highest?

_____

2. When was it the lowest?

_____

3. Why do you think this was so?

_____

Tool: Fahrenheit thermometer

Unit 5 Assessment
Mass

Look at each picture. Darken the circle by the correct answer.

1.

Ⓐ 2 pounds
Ⓑ 2 ounces
Ⓒ 2 tons

2.

Ⓐ 2 ounces
Ⓑ 2 tons
Ⓒ 2 pounds

3.

Ⓐ 3 ounces
Ⓑ 3 pounds
Ⓒ 3 tons

4.

Ⓐ 6 tons
Ⓑ 6 ounces
Ⓒ 6 pounds

Go on to the next page.

Unit 5 Assessment
Mass, p. 2

DIRECTIONS

Read each question. Darken the circle by the correct answer.

5. Last year Jack weighed 35 pounds. This year he weighs 41 pounds. How much weight did Jack gain?

  Ⓐ 5 pounds

  Ⓑ 4 pounds

  Ⓒ 6 pounds

6. Susan's shelf can hold 2 pounds. Her dolls weigh 8 ounces each. How many dolls can Susan put on her shelf?

  Ⓐ 2 dolls

  Ⓑ 4 dolls

  Ⓒ 6 dolls

7. Bob's dog weighs 8 pounds. Rick's dog weighs half as much as Bob's dog. How much does Rick's dog weigh?

  Ⓐ 4 ounces

  Ⓑ 2 pounds

  Ⓒ 4 pounds

8. Kim wants to buy 4 kilograms of beans. Each bag weighs 2 kilograms. How many bags should she buy?

  Ⓐ 5 bags

  Ⓑ 1 bag

  Ⓒ 2 bags

Name _____ Date _____

"Weight" for Me!

DIRECTIONS

Circle the one that weighs more.

1.

2.

3.

DIRECTIONS

Circle the objects that weigh less than you weigh.

4.

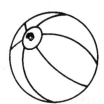  

Kilogram Weight

Circle the better estimate.

1.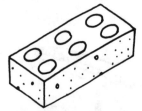

2 kilograms
20 kilograms

2.

1 kilogram
10 kilograms

3.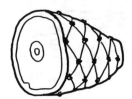

4 kilograms
40 kilograms

4.

1 kilogram
10 kilograms

Write a number sentence, and solve this problem.

5. Tim buys 4 kilograms of apples. He uses about 2 kilograms of apples to bake a pie. About how many kilograms of apples does he have left?

_____ about _____ kilograms

Match 'em Up!

DIRECTIONS

Draw a line from each picture to its weight.

1. 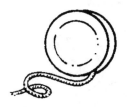   **a.** 6 pounds

2.    **b.** 15 pounds

3.    **c.** 2 ounces

4.    **d.** 2 tons

5.    **e.** 3 pounds

Name _____   Date _____

Cozy Cats

DIRECTIONS
Look at the cats. Each cat is sitting on a scale. Answer the questions below the cats.

1. Which cat weighs the most?

_____

2. Which cat weighs the least?

_____

3. There is a _____ kg difference between Minnie and Red.

_____

4. Which cat weighs more than 2 other cats together?

_____

5. Which 2 cats weigh the same amount?

_____

6. Write each cat's name in order from the lightest to the heaviest.

_____

_____

Name _____ Date _____

On the Balance

DIRECTIONS

Choose 5 school tools, such as crayons, scissors, or glue. Using only a balance, find which item weighs the most. Which item weighs the least? List the items in order from the heaviest to the lightest.

1.

2.

3.

4.

5.

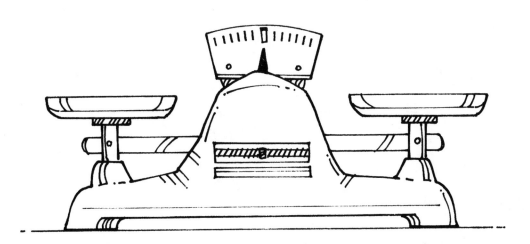

Tools: balance, various objects to weigh

Package Pounds

DIRECTIONS

You want to send a package to a friend. Imagine 5 things you would like to send. List them below. How much do you think each item would weigh? How much would it cost to send your package?

WINDOW NO. 3	PACKAGE RATES	
	POUNDS	COST
	0 - 5	$2
	5 - 10	$3
	10 - 15	$4
	15 - 20	$5
	20 - 30	$7
	30 - 40	$9

ZIP CODE YOUR MAIL

NEW STAMP RATES

STAMPS

Items	**Weights**
1. _____	_____
2. _____	_____
3. _____	_____
4. _____	_____
5. _____	_____

Total weight _____

Cost to send _____

Hint: Remember, 16 ounces = 1 pound.

Name _____ Date _____

Unit 6 Assessment
Time

DIRECTIONS
Look at the clocks. Darken the circle by the correct time.

1.

Ⓐ 5:00

Ⓑ 6:00

Ⓒ 5:30

2.

Ⓐ 2:15

Ⓑ 3:15

Ⓒ 2:30

3.

Ⓐ 8:00

Ⓑ 8:15

Ⓒ 9:15

4.

3:30

Ⓐ 3 o'clock

Ⓑ 30 minutes after 3

Ⓒ 15 minutes after 3

Go on to the next page.

Unit 6 Assessment
Time, p. 2

DIRECTIONS

Read each question. Draw hands on the alarm clock to help find the answer. Darken the circle by the correct answer.

5. What time is it 15 minutes after 2:00?

Ⓐ 2:30

Ⓑ 2:15

Ⓒ 3:00

6. What time is it 4 hours after 10:30?

Ⓐ 3:00

Ⓑ 3:30

Ⓒ 2:30

7. What time is it one half hour before 6:30?

Ⓐ 6:00

Ⓑ 7:00

Ⓒ 5:30

8. What time is it 15 minutes after 11:45?

Ⓐ 11:30

Ⓑ 10:00

Ⓒ 12:00

Talking Time

About how long will it take? Circle the better estimate.

1.

to drink a glass of water

1 minute   1 hour

2.

to play a game

1 minute   1 hour

3.

to yawn

1 minute   1 hour

4.

to fix dinner

1 minute   1 hour

Solve this problem.

5. It is 3:30. Chan has a piano lesson at 4:00.
Does Chan have time to see a movie?
Circle <u>Yes</u> or <u>No</u>.

Yes   No

Name _____   Date _____

James's Jobs

On Saturday morning, James's father told him to

do his homework at 9:30.   wake up at 8:00.

help with shopping at 11:00.   empty the trash at 9:00.

clean his room at 8:30   mail a letter at 10:30.

DIRECTIONS

Write the correct time. Then, number the pictures to show the order.

1.

DIRECTIONS

Answer the question.

2. After what time can James play?

_____

Name _____ Date _____

Time for Thomas

Thomas has things to do after breakfast. The bus leaves in 15 minutes. Will he have time to do everything and also catch the bus? Use this chart to answer the questions.

Walk the dog	3 minutes	Make the bed	2 minutes
Feed the dog	3 minutes	Pack books	1 minute
Pack up lunch	2 minutes	Walk to the bus stop	2 minutes

A. How much time do these things take? _____ minutes

B. Does Thomas have enough time to catch the bus? _____

C. How much time is left? _____ minutes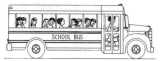

Write 6 things you do before you leave for school. Tell how much time each one takes.

1. _____ _____ minutes   **2.** _____ _____ minutes

3. _____ _____ minutes   **4.** _____ _____ minutes

5. _____ _____ minutes   **6.** _____ _____ minutes

How Many Minutes?

Each clock is shaded to show a part of an hour. Look at the shaded part of each clock. Then answer the questions.

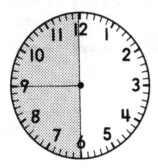
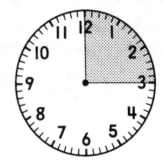

1. Look at the clock that shows 2 quarters. Color another quarter of an hour. How many minutes is this?

_____

2. Look at the clock that shows 1 quarter. Shade another quarter of an hour. How many minutes is this?

_____

3. Look at the clock that is not shaded. Color a half hour. How many minutes is this?

_____

4. Look at the clock that shows 3 quarters. Shade another quarter of an hour. How many minutes is this?

_____

A Handy Clock

DIRECTIONS

Make a clock. You will need:

a paper plate   colored paper   inch ruler
a fastener   a marker

A. Draw 2 clock hands on the colored paper. Make the minute hand 5 inches long. Make the hour hand 3 inches long. Cut out the hands.

B. The paper plate is the clock face. Write the hours on the clock with <u>12</u> at the top and <u>6</u> at the bottom. Look at your classroom clock or the one above.

C. Attach the hands to the center of the plate with the fastener.

DIRECTIONS

Use your clock to answer these questions.

1. Show where your clock hands would be at 12:00.

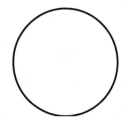

2. Show your clock hands 3 hours later.

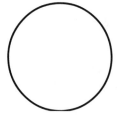

3. Show where your clock hands would be at 5:15.

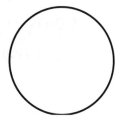

4. Show where your clock hands would be 30 minutes later.

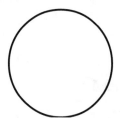

Tools: colored paper, paper plate, fastener, inch ruler, marker

Helpful Hands

DIRECTIONS
Write the time. Draw hands on the clocks to show the time.

1.

What is the
time now?

_____

2.

What was the time
30 minutes ago?

_____

3.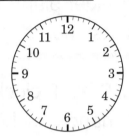

What will the time
be 30 minutes
from now?

_____

4.

What is the
time now?

_____

5.

What was the time
30 minutes ago?

_____

6.

What will the time
be 30 minutes
from now?

_____

7.

8:00

What is the
time now?

_____

8.

What was the time
2 hours ago?

_____

9.

What will the time
be 4 hours
from now?

_____

64

Hour Power

DIRECTIONS
Draw the hour hand to show the time.

1.

5:00

2.

8:00

DIRECTIONS
Draw the hour hand and the minute hand to show the time.

3.

12:00

4.

9:00

5.

1:00

DIRECTIONS
Draw hands on the clock to show 1 hour later.

6. 1:00

7. 10:00

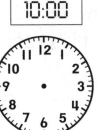

8. 11:00

DIRECTIONS
Solve this problem.

9. The bus leaves in 1 hour. It is 2:00 now.
What time will the bus leave? _____:_____

Name _____ Date _____

Busy Bob

DIRECTIONS

This is how Bob spends his day. Use the pictograph to answer the questions.

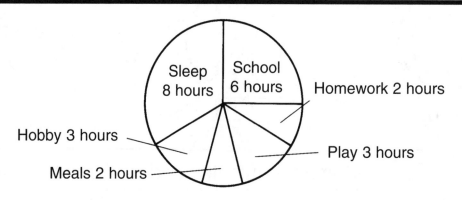

1. What takes the longest time?

_____

2. How many hours does Bob spend eating?

_____

3. What takes the same amount of time as homework?

_____

4. What lasts 6 hours?

_____

5. Make a pictograph to show the same facts shown on the pie graph.

	◯ = 1 hour		
Play	◯◯◯		
Meals			
Hobby			
Homework			
School			
Sleep			

Problem Time

DIRECTIONS

Solve these problems.

August

Sun	Mon	Tues	Wed	Thur	Fri	Sat
			1	2	3	4
5	6	7	8	9	10	11
12	13	14	15	16	17	18
19	20	21	22	23	24	25
26	27	28	29	30	31	

1. Dee goes to camp the third Friday in August. Circle that date on the calendar.

2. Dee's airplane leaves at 3:00. Draw the hands on the clock to show the time the airplane leaves.

3. About how long will the airplane trip take? Circle the better estimate.

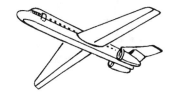

1 minute   1 hour

4. When the airplane lands, the clock shows this time. Write the time.

_____:_____

Name _____   Date _____

A Busy Month

DIRECTIONS

Write the dates on the calendar. Then, use the calendar to answer the questions.

1. Place each letter on the calendar.

a. Mother's birthday, June 20   **b.** Ellie's play, June 4

c. softball game, second Tuesday   **d.** camp picnic, third Saturday

e. family trip, Saturday after Mother's birthday   **f.** Uncle's visit, fifth Wednesday

June						
Sun.	Mon.	Tues.	Wed.	Thurs.	Fri.	Sat.
		1	2	3	4	5
6	7	8	9	10	11	12
13	14	15	16	17	18	19
20a	21	22	23	24	25	26
27	28	29	30			

2. What happened first: the family trip or Mother's birthday?

_____

3. What event happened next after Ellie's play?

_____

4. What happened last: Uncle's visit or the camp picnic?

_____

5. Skip-count by 2's, and circle every day Ellie goes to the park. Ellie does not go to the park on the days she has other plans.

_____

Name _____ Date _____

Bedtime

DIRECTIONS

What must you do before going to bed each night? How long do you think each activity takes? Look at a clock to help you fill in the chart.

Activity	Time

DIRECTIONS

Now, think about the time you should be in bed. Using the above table, what time should you start to get ready for bed?

My bedtime is _____.

I should start to get ready for bed at _____.

Tool: clock

Name _____ Date _____

A Great Day

If you could plan your next Saturday in any way you liked, how would you do it? What would you do first? How would you end the day? Make a schedule to show the perfect day. Write the time for each activity.

Unit 7 Assessment
Money

Look at each group of coins. Darken the circle by the correct amount.

1.

   Ⓐ 50 cents

   Ⓑ 40 cents

   Ⓒ 35 cents

2.

   Ⓐ 52 cents

   Ⓑ 42 cents

   Ⓒ 47 cents

3.

   Ⓐ 30 cents

   Ⓑ 85 cents

   Ⓒ 25 cents

4.

   Ⓐ 18 cents

   Ⓑ 13 cents

   Ⓒ 25 cents

Go on to the next page.

Unit 7 Assessment
Money, p. 2

5. Joe has 75¢. He buys this bag of marbles. How much does he have left?

  Ⓐ 25¢

  Ⓑ 35¢

  Ⓒ 40¢

6. Tess wants to buy 2 of these bananas. How much money does she need?

  Ⓐ 50¢

  Ⓑ 15¢

  Ⓒ 26¢

7. Jill has 2 quarters. Does she have enough money to buy this flower for her mother?

  Ⓐ No, she needs more money.

  Ⓑ Yes, she has more than she needs.

  Ⓒ Yes, she has just the right amount.

8. Andy wants to buy this airplane. Which coins could he use?

  Ⓐ 1 quarter and 5 pennies

  Ⓑ 2 dimes and 3 nickels

  Ⓒ 1 dime, 2 nickels, and 5 pennies

Counting Coins

Count on to find the total amount.

1.

<u> 5 </u> ¢   <u> 10 </u> ¢   <u> 15 </u> ¢   <u> 16 </u> ¢ | 16 | ¢

2.

____ ¢   ____ ¢   ____ ¢   ____ ¢ | | ¢

3.

____ ¢   ____ ¢   ____ ¢   ____ ¢   ____ ¢ | | ¢

4.

____ ¢   ____ ¢   ____ ¢   ____ ¢   ____ ¢   ____ ¢ | | ¢

Solve this problem.

5. Robert has 4 nickels and 3 pennies.
Can he buy the grapes? Circle <u>Yes</u> or <u>No</u>.

Yes   No

Which Is More?

Count on to find the total amounts. Circle the greater amount.

1.

___31___ ¢   (36) ¢

2.

_____ ¢   _____ ¢

3.

_____ ¢   _____ ¢

Solve this problem.

4. Len has 24¢.
Tina has 44¢.
Who can buy the toy?

35¢

_____

How Much Is Left?

Count up from the price to find the change.

1. You have 70¢.
You buy

59¢ _60_ ¢ _70_ ¢
You have __12_ ¢ change.

2. You have 45¢.
You buy

39¢ ____ ¢ ____ ¢
You have ____¢ change.

3. You have 65¢.
You buy

53¢ ____ ¢ ____ ¢ ____ ¢
You have ____¢ change.

Write a number sentence, and solve.

4. Janine has 50¢ to spend. She buys a daisy
for 24¢. How much change will she get back?

_____   _____¢

At the Toy Store

DIRECTIONS

Use the pictures to solve.

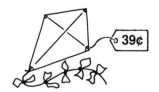  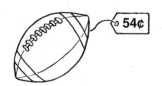 

1. Kim bought a football and a kite.
   How much did she spend? __93__ ¢
   Show your work.

   ```
     54 ¢
   + 39 ¢
     93 ¢
   ```

2. Ms. Tuma bought a kite and a dinosaur.
   How much did she spend? _____¢
   Show your work.

   ```
       _____¢
   +   _____¢
       _____¢
   ```

3. Carlos spent more than 60¢ on 1 toy.
   Which toy did he buy? Circle the answer.

   kite   dinosaur   football   yo-yo

4. Mark has 95¢. He wants to buy a yo-yo and a kite.
   Does he have enough money? Circle <u>Yes</u> or <u>No</u>.

   Yes   No

Fair Fare

At the Spring County Fair, the children sold lunches.
Use the menu to make up a question. Then solve.

Menu

Juices		Sandwiches	
Tomato	25¢	Chicken	55¢
Orange	35¢	Cheese	40¢
Grape	30¢	Ham	60¢
		Sandwiches with tomato: 10¢ extra.	

1. Rita buys grape juice and a ham sandwich.

__How much does__

__she spend?__

Solve: _____ 90¢ _____

2. Ken has 90¢. He buys a ham sandwich. He wants juice, too.

_____

_____

Solve: _____

3. Chita buys a chicken sandwich. Lois buys a cheese sandwich with tomato.

_____

_____

Solve: _____

4. Mr. Wu buys tomato juice for his son and orange juice for his daughter.

_____

_____

Solve: _____

Paper Pay

Heather and Eddie deliver papers. For every Eddie earns, Heather earns .
For every Eddie earns, Heather earns 👛👛 .

DIRECTIONS

Use play money to help you answer these questions.

1. If Eddie earns 25 cents, how much does Heather earn?

_____

2. If Heather earns $1.00, how much does Eddie earn?

_____

3. Heather and Eddie earned $3.00 altogether one week. How much did each child earn?

_____

4. If Eddie earns 60 cents, how much does Heather earn?

_____

5. The chart shows the money the children earned in 1 month. Write the missing numbers. Add to find the totals.

	Heather	Eddie
First week		$0.45
Second week	$0.60	
Third week	$1.40	$0.70
Fourth week		$0.60
Total		

Name _____ Date _____

Lucky Lemons

DIRECTIONS
Jane and Toby are selling lemonade.
Use this sign to answer the questions.

Lemonade 10¢ a Cup

LEMONADE RECIPE	SHOPPING LIST
2 cups sugar	Lemons 25¢ each
4 lemons	Sugar 15¢ a cup
64 ounces of ice water	Cups 2¢ each
Recipe makes 20 cups	

1. How much will it cost to make a
pitcher of lemonade?

lemons ___$1.00___

sugar _____

total _____

2. How much will the cups for a pitcher
of lemonade cost?

_____

3. What is the cost of the lemonade and
the cups?

_____

4. If Jane and Toby sell 20 cups, how much
money do they take in?

_____

5. Do they make more than they spend?

_____

If yes, how much more?

_____

Use Your Common "Cents"

DIRECTIONS
Solve these problems.

1. Mae has 1 quarter and 4 nickels in her bank. She adds 1 dime. How much money does Mae have in her bank?

_____ ¢

2. Tran has 58¢ in all. What coins are left in her purse? Write how many. Circle the coin name.

_____ dimes   nickels   pennies

3. You have

Do you have enough money to buy a  Circle Yes or No.

Yes   No

4. Which amount could you make with the fewest coins? Circle the amount.

41¢   51¢   61¢

Way to Pay

DIRECTIONS

Look in newspaper ads and catalogs for something you would like to buy.

I want to buy _____.

It costs _____.

List 4 different combinations of coins and bills you can use to pay for the item. Use play money to help find the combinations.

Tools: newspaper or catalogs; play money

Name _____ Date _____

A Hamster Home

DIRECTIONS

Suppose you wanted a hamster. How much money would you need to buy the hamster's food and shavings? What else would you need? Write what you think it would cost in the chart. Then, go to a pet store with an adult. Write the costs in the chart. How close were you?

Cost of Having a Hamster

	Your Estimate	Pet Store Cost
Hamster		
Cage		
Shavings		
Food		
Treats		
Other		
Totals		

Name _____ Date _____

Unit 8 Assessment
Computation

DIRECTIONS

Add the lengths. Write the perimeter.

1.

2 cm

1 cm [ ] 1 cm

2 cm

_____ + _____ + _____ + _____ = _____ cm

2.

3 cm

1 cm [ ] 1 cm

3 cm

_____ + _____ + _____ + _____ = _____ cm

DIRECTIONS

Use your inch ruler. Find the perimeter.

3.

_____ + _____ + _____ = _____ inches

4.

_____ + _____ + _____ + _____ = _____ inches

DIRECTIONS

Count the square units. Write the number of square centimeters.

5.

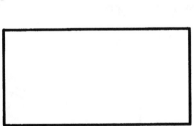

_____ square centimeters

6.

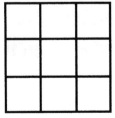

_____ square centimeters

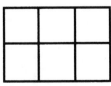
Tools: inch ruler

Go on to the next page.

Unit 8 Assessment
Computation, p. 2

DIRECTIONS

Read each problem. Darken the circle by the correct answer.

7. Diego's room has 4 walls. Each wall is 10 feet long. What is the perimeter of Diego's room?

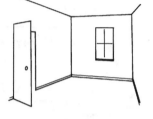

  Ⓐ 20 feet

  Ⓑ 40 feet

  Ⓒ 10 feet

8. Tina's book is 9 inches long. It is 6 inches wide. What is the perimeter of Tina's book?

  Ⓐ 30 inches

  Ⓑ 18 inches

  Ⓒ 15 inches

9. John has 3 pencils. Each pencil is 8 centimeters long. He has his pencils in the shape of a triangle. What is the perimeter of the triangle?

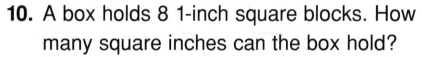

  Ⓐ 8 centimeters

  Ⓑ 32 centimeters

  Ⓒ 24 centimeters

10. A box holds 8 1-inch square blocks. How many square inches can the box hold?

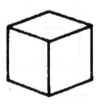

  Ⓐ 1

  Ⓑ 8

  Ⓒ 4

Name _____ Date _____

All the Way Around

2 in.

1 in.   1 in.

2 in.

1 + 2 + 1 + 2 = 6 in.

Add the lengths of the sides to find the perimeter.

DIRECTIONS

Measure the sides of each figure in inches. Find the perimeter. Write the number of inches.

1.

_1_ + _1_ + _1_ = _3_ in.

2.

____ + ____ + ____ + ____ = ____ in.

3.

____ + ____ + ____ + ____ = ____ in.

4.

____ + ____ + ____ = ____ in.

Tool: inch ruler

Unit 8: Computation: Perimeter
Measurement 2, SV 2066-4

Add 'em Up

To find the perimeter of a shape, measure each side. Then, add the lengths of the sides.

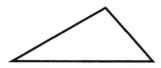

3 cm + 2 cm + 4 cm = 9 cm

The perimeter is 9 cm.

DIRECTIONS

Use your centimeter ruler. Measure each side. Add the lengths.

1.

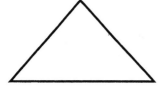

_____ + _____ + _____ = _____ cm

2.

_____ + _____ + _____ + _____ = _____ cm

3.

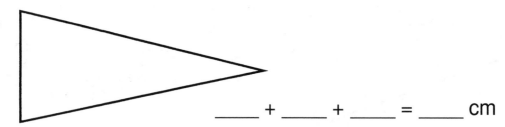

_____ + _____ + _____ = _____ cm

Tool: centimeter ruler

Use a Scale

In this rectangle, each ☐ is 50 feet on each side.

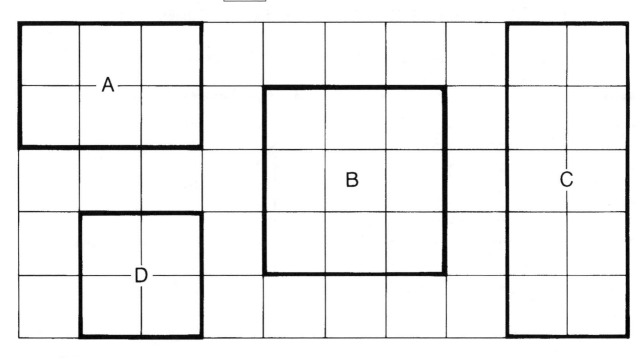

DIRECTIONS

Look at each shape. Count and add, then write the answer.

1. What is the distance around A?

_____

2. What is the distance around B?

_____

3. What is the distance around C?

_____

4. What is the distance around D?

_____

A Helpful Tool

DIRECTIONS

Use a centimeter ruler to measure each shape.

Use a to find the perimeter. Write the perimeter.

1.

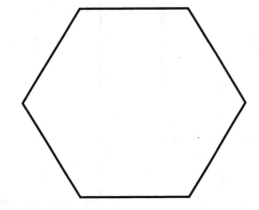

_____ centimeters

2.

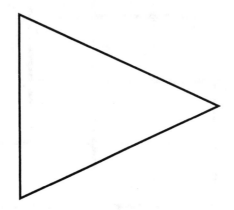

_____ centimeters

3.

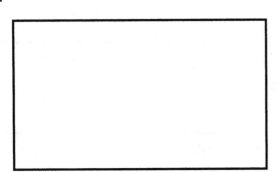

_____ centimeters

4.

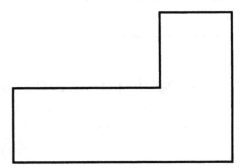

_____ centimeters

Tools: centimeter ruler, calculator

Name _____ Date _____

Lettuce See...

DIRECTIONS

Every 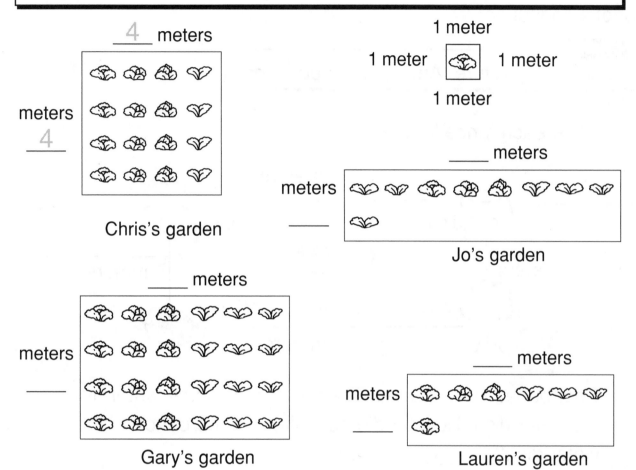 needs land that is 1 meter on each side. Look at the pictures. Answer the questions.

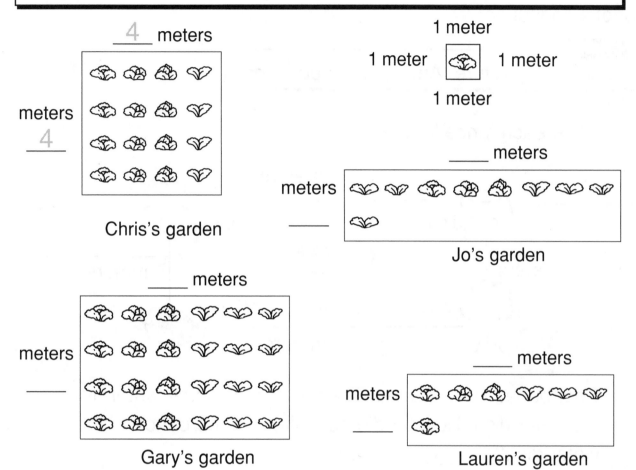

_4_ meters

meters
_4_

Chris's garden

1 meter
1 meter [ ] 1 meter
1 meter

_____ meters

meters
_____

Jo's garden

_____ meters

meters
_____

Gary's garden

_____ meters

meters
_____

Lauren's garden

1. Write the meters on each side of the gardens.

2. Draw the rest of the 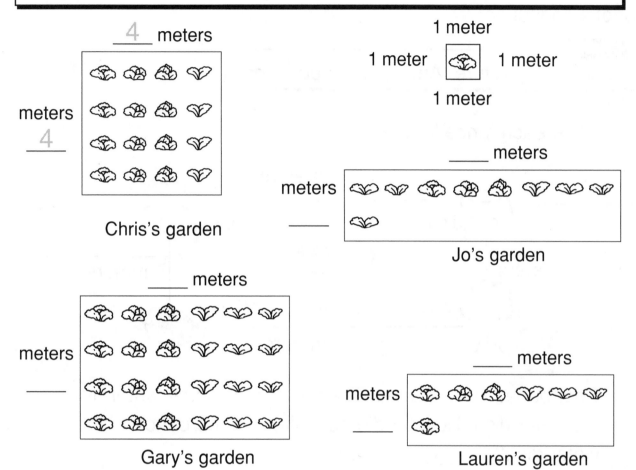 in each garden.

Add the sides of each garden. Write the perimeter.

3. Chris's garden __16__ meters   **4.** Lauren's garden _____ meters

5. Gary's garden _____ meters   **6.** Jo's garden _____ meters

7. Whose garden has the most plants? _____

Spot's Space

There is a fence around Spot's backyard. The tree is 5 meters away from Spot's water dish. The tree is 7 meters away from Spot's doghouse.

DIRECTIONS

Look at the picture. Answer the questions.

1. Write each fence length.

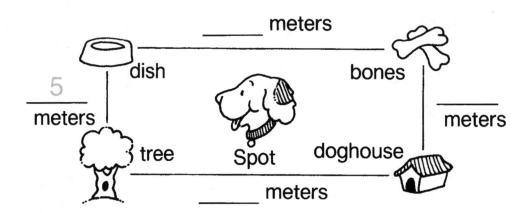

2. Spot buried some bones. Then, he drank some water from his water dish. How far did he walk from the bones to the water dish? _____ meters

3. Later, Spot walked from his doghouse back to where the bones were buried. How far did he walk? _____ meters

4. What numbers would you add to show how far it is around Spot's yard?

___7___ + _____ + _____ + _____

5. How many meters is it around Spot's yard? _____ meters

Name _____ Date _____

Square Inches

Count square inches to find the area of a shape.

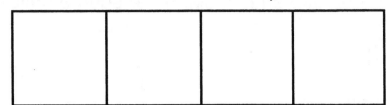

1 square inch   4 square inches

DIRECTIONS

Write the number of square inches.
Check your work with 1-inch counting cubes.

1.

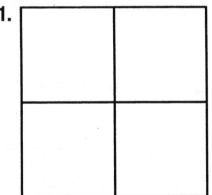

_____ square inches

2.

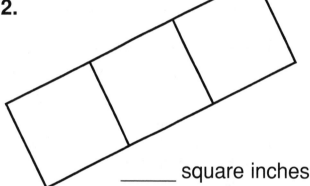

_____ square inches

3.

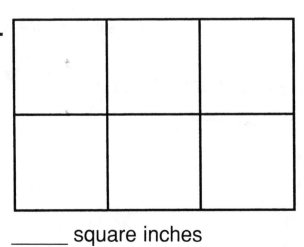

_____ square inches

4.

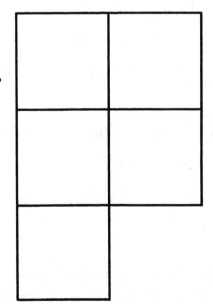

_____ square inches

Tool: 1-inch counting cubes

Square Centimeters

To find the area of a shape, count the square units.

1 square centimeter

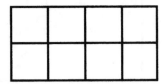

8 square centimeters

DIRECTIONS
Write the number of square centimeters.

1.

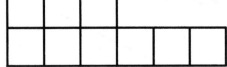

_____ square centimeters

2.

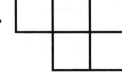

_____ square centimeters

3.

_____ square centimeters

4.

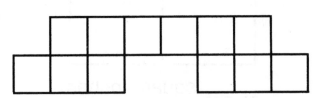

_____ square centimeters

5. Make 3 shapes on centimeter graph paper. Swap shapes with a partner. Write the number of square centimeters for each shape.

Tool: centimeter graph paper

Size Wise

Count the square inches to find the area. Write the number of square inches. Check your work with an inch ruler.

1.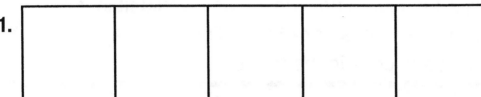

square inches

_____

2.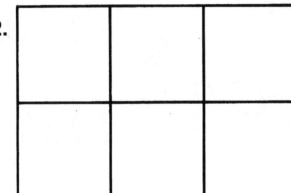

_____ square inches

3.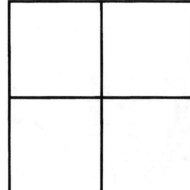

_____ square inches

Write the number of square centimeters for each. Check your work with a centimeter ruler.

4.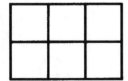

_____ square centimeters

5.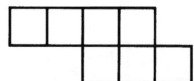

_____ square centimeters

Tools: inch ruler and centimeter ruler

A Mix of Measures

DIRECTIONS

How could you measure your classroom without using a ruler? How long is your classroom? How wide is your classroom? If your desk were a square unit, how many would fit in your classroom? Imagine them stacked up, filling all the space in the room. Write your ideas in the frame.

Measurement: Grade 2

Answer Key

Pp. 9–12
Overall Assessment

1. B	13. C
2. A	14. A
3. B	15. C
4. C	16. B
5. B	17. A
6. B	18. C
7. A	19. B
8. B	20. C
9. A	21. A
10. C	22. C
11. A	23. A
12. B	24. C

Pp. 13–14
Unit 1 Assessment

1. B	5. A
2. C	6. C
3. B	7. C
4. B	8. B

P. 15
1. c
2. a
3. d
4. b

P. 16
1. B	3. More
2. coat	4. No

P. 17
1. about 10 minutes
2. more than 1 hour
3. about 1 hour or more than 1 hour
4. about 10 minutes
5. about 1 hour
6. about 10 minutes

P. 18
2. >500	6. >400
3. >500	7. <600
4. <900	8. <800
5. >800	

P. 19
1. 10	3. 6
2. 6	

Pp. 21–22
Unit 2 Assessment

1. B	5. C
2. A	6. B
3. A	7. A
4. B	8. B

Pp. 23–24
A. 1/4 inch
B. 1/2 inch
C. 1 3/4 inches
D. 3 inches
E. 4 3/4 inches
F. 5 1/2 inches
1. 2 1/4 inches
2. 1 1/2 inches
3. 2 inches
4. 1 1/2 inches
5. 2 inches
6. 1 1/2 inches
7. 4 1/4 inches
8. 1 3/4 inches
9. 1 1/4 inches
10. 5 inches

P. 25
1. 2 inches
2. 1 1/2 inches
3. 1 inch
4. 2 1/2 inches
5. 3 1/4 inches

P. 26
1–3. Answers will vary.
Estimates:
1. 10 inches
2. 2 inches
3. 5 inches
4. Yes

P. 27
1. 3
2. 5
3. 4
4. 2
5. First box should be circled.

P. 28
Check students' work.

P. 29
1–3. Check students' work.
4. 12 + 12 = 24; 24 centimeters

P. 30
2. at 90 feet
3. 20 feet
4. at 50 feet
5. 60 feet
6. 70 feet

P. 31
Answers may vary slightly.
1. 250 feet
2. 325 feet
3. 350 feet
4. 125 feet
5. 100 feet

Pp. 33–34
Unit 3 Assessment

1. A	5. C
2. B	6. A
3. C	7. C
4. B	8. C

P. 35
1. 2	6. 3
2. 2	7. 8
3. 4	8. 4
4. 2	9. 4
5. 16	10. 2

P. 36
1. less than 1 quart
2. about 1 gallon
3. color 2 cups
4. color 4 cups
5. 4

P. 37
1. 2, 1; 2, 1; 4, 1
2. b
3. a
4. a
5. b

P. 38
1. 1,000
2. 500
3. 2,000
4. 250
5. Answers will vary
6. mL
7. L
8. mL
9. mL
10. kL
11. L

P. 39
1. 3	3. 1
2. 3	4. 1

Pp. 41–42
Unit 4 Assessment

1. B	5. C
2. A	6. B
3. C	7. A
4. B	8. B

P. 43
1. 30 degrees Fahrenheit
2. 90 degrees Fahrenheit
3. 70 degrees Fahrenheit
4. 50 degrees Fahrenheit
5. Answers will vary.

Pp. 44–45
Answers will vary. Check for reasonable activities. Check thermometers for correct temperatures.

P. 46
Check students' graphs.
1. Monday
2. Thursday
3. Wednesday

P. 47
1. High Temperatures
2. 5
3. May
4. July
5. 20 degrees
6. 50 degrees

P. 48
Charts will vary. Check students' work.

Pp. 49–50
Unit 5 Assessment

1. A	5. C
2. B	6. B
3. A	7. C
4. C	8. C

P. 51
1. airplane
2. ship
3. bus
4. beach ball; rabbit

P. 52
1. 2 kilograms
2. 1 kilogram
3. 4 kilograms
4. 10 kilograms
5. 4 − 2 = 2; about 2 kilograms

Measurement 2, SV 2066-4

P. 53
1. c   4. a
2. d   5. b
3. e

P. 54
1. Minnie
2. Red
3. 5
4. Minnie
5. Solo and Tiger
6. Red, Solo and Tiger, Jacks, Dancer, Minnie

P. 55
Answers will vary. Check students' results.

Pp. 57–58
Unit 6 Assessment
1. C   5. B
2. A   6. C
3. B   7. A
4. B   8. C

P. 59
1. 1 minute
2. 1 hour
3. 1 minute
4. 1 hour
5. No

P. 60
1. In order from sending a letter and clockwise: 10:30; 9:00; 9:30; 8:30; 8:00; 11:00 Pictures should be numbered 1-6 in this order: 1. wake up; 2. clean room; 3. empty trash; 4. do homework; 5. mail letter; 6. help with shopping
2. Answers may vary. After shopping, around 11:30 or 12:00; or after lunch, around 12:30 or 1:00.

P. 61
A. 13
B. yes
C. 2
1–6. Answers will vary.

P. 62
Check students' clocks.
1. 45 minutes
2. 30 minutes
3. 30 minutes
4. 60 minutes

P. 63
Check students' work.
1. clock hands at 12:00
2. clock hands at 3:00
3. clock hands at 5:15
4. clock hands at 5:45

P. 64
1. 4:00   6. 1:00
2. 3:30   7. 8:00
3. 4:30   8. 6:00
4. 12:30   9. 12:00
5. 12:00

P. 65
2. hour hand on 8
3. both hands on 12
4. minute hand on 12; hour hand on 9
5. minute hand on 12; hour hand on 1
6. minute hand on 12; hour hand on 2
7. minute hand on 12; hour hand on 11
8. both hands on 12
9. 3:00

P. 66
1. sleep
2. 2 hours
3. eating
4. school
5. Meals, 2 circles; Hobby, 3 circles; Homework, 2 circles; School, 6 circles; Sleep, 8 circles

P. 67
1. circle 17th
2. minute hand on the 12; hour hand on the 3
3. 1 hour
4. 3:45

P. 68
1. a on June 20; b on June 4; c on June 8; d on June 19; e on June 26; f on June 30
2. Mother's birthday
3. softball game
4. Uncle's visit
5. circle 2, 6, 10, 12, 14, 16, 18, 22, 24, and 28

Pp. 71–72
Unit 7 Assessment
1. B   5. B
2. A   6. C
3. C   7. C
4. A   8. B

P. 73
2. 10, 20, 30, 31; 31¢
3. 10, 15, 20, 25, 26; 26¢
4. 10, 20, 30, 40, 45, 46; 46¢
5. Yes

P. 74
2. 35; 27; circle 35
3. 40; 41; circle 41
4. Tina

P. 75
2. 40, 45; 7
3. 54, 55, 65; 13
4. 50 − 24 = 26; 26

P. 76
2. 83; 39 + 44 = 83
3. yo-yo
4. No

P. 77
Questions may vary.
2. Which kind of juice can he buy?; tomato or grape juice
3. Who spends more?; Chita
4. How much does he spend?; 60¢

P. 78
1. 50 cents
2. 50 cents
3. Heather earned $2.00, and Eddie earned $1.00.
4. $1.20
5. First week, $0.90; Second week, $0.30; Fourth week, $1.20; Totals: Heather, $4.10; Eddie, $2.05

P. 79
1. sugar, 30¢; total, $1.30
2. 40¢
3. $1.70
4. $2.00
5. Yes; 30¢

P. 80
1. 55
2. 3 pennies
3. No
4. 51¢; 2 quarters and 1 penny or 1 half-dollar and 1 penny

Pp. 83–84
Unit 8 Assessment
1. 1 + 2 + 1 + 2 = 6 cm
2. 1 + 3 + 1 + 3 = 8 cm
3. 2 + 2 + 1 = 5 inches
4. 1 + 2 + 1 + 2 = 6 inches

5. 6   8. A
6. 9   9. C
7. B   10. B

P. 85
2. 2 + 2 + 2 + 2 = 8
3. 1 + 3 + 1 + 3 = 8
4. 1 + 3 + 3 = 7

P. 86
1. 3 + 3 + 4 = 10
2. 3 + 3 + 3 + 3 = 12
3. 3 + 7 + 7 = 17

P. 87
1. 500 feet
2. 600 feet
3. 700 feet
4. 400 feet

P. 88
1. 18
2. 17
3. 22
4. 20

P. 89
1. Lauren's garden, 6 x 2; Gary's garden, 6 x 4; Jo's garden, 8 x 2
2. Check students' work.
3. 16
4. 16
5. 20
6. 20
7. Gary's

P. 90
1. Fence is 7 meters by 5 meters.
2. 7
3. 5
4. 7 + 5 + 7 + 5
5. 24

P. 91
1. 4   3. 6
2. 3   4. 5

P. 92
1. 9
2. 4
3. 12
4. 12
5. Drawings will vary. Check results.

P. 93
1. 5   4. 6
2. 5   5. 7
3. 3